Henry Green

by ROBERT S. RYF

Columbia University Press
NEW YORK & LONDON 1967

COLUMBIA ESSAYS ON MODERN WRITERS is a series of critical studies of English, Continental, and other writers whose works are of contemporary artistic and intellectual significance.

Editor: William York Tindall

Advisory Editors

Jacques Barzun   W. T. H. Jackson   Joseph A. Mazzeo   Justin O'Brien

Henry Green is Number 29 of the series.

ROBERT S. RYF is Professor of English and Comparative Literature and Dean of the Faculty at Occidental College. He is the author of *A New Approach to Joyce.*

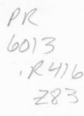
Grateful acknowledgment is made to Henry Green and to his publishers, the Hogarth Press, Ltd., and the Viking Press, Inc., for permission to quote passages from his published works: *Blindness, Living, Party Going, Pack My Bag, Caught, Loving, Back, Concluding, Nothing,* and *Doting;* and also to The Macmillan Company for permission to quote from *Living.*

Henry Green

Nearly everyone who writes about Henry Green ends up calling him elusive. Nearly everyone who reads him understands why. Trying to come to discursive grips with his novels is rather like trying to pluck and pocket smoke rings; the attempt yields intimations of design, evanescent luminosities and pervasive fragrance, but precious little palpable residue.

Initially, our situation as we prowl through his verbal fugues attempting to pounce on meaning seems not unlike that of the cat who, entering the barn a moment too late, almost saw the mouse. But mice, although properly elusive, are not suitable symbols of significance in Green; birds are better. Whether on the wing, sitting, or dead, their presence in Green's novels seems somehow (and how that word hovers over one when thinking about Green!) to inform and order them, their swift elusive flights to suggest the delicate play of motifs, their occasional flocking the subtle clusterings of meaning. They both connect and spin off motifs, and contemplating their place in Green's ambiguous fictional world, one understands the plight of that speaker in one of Wallace Stevens's poems about complexity, who was finally astonished to discover that fluttering things have so distinct a shade.

Green's fluttering novels have been variously perceived and assessed. His work has been described as ambiguous, enigmatic, cryptic, excessively mannered, and brilliant. Green himself has done little to illuminate the enigmas which envelope him and his work. Like Wallace Stevens, he has led two lives, and they seem not to have overlapped appreciably. An industrialist now retired, he has, in the past, written and said very little publicly about his work or that of other writers. His most recent published word to the outside world is suitably cryptic: he advises people in general to stay home, preferably in bed. While there seems little disagreement as to his importance or talent, there is considerably more as to the nature and beneficence of his influence. On the one hand, he is regarded as one of the central symbolist novelists of our time, in the tradition of Conrad, Joyce, and Virginia Woolf, one who has made important innovations in the modern novel. On the other hand, he has been condemned as a slick and decadent fooler-around with words and techniques, one whose verbal pyrotechnics, while dazzling, have cast their garish light along quite the wrong path for the novel to take.

I undo and spread this bundle of controversy simply to provide a context rather than to argue either case, for my focus will be on what has been written *by*, rather than *about*, Green. And that provides task enough. Clearly, Green's novels pose more puzzles than can be parsed in one essay. My aim, therefore, is finite, my method inductive. I will examine the books in chronological order, trapping meaning where I can, and drawing such conclusions as seem appropriate. At the end, I will attempt a few generalizations which seem called for, or at least within hailing distance, about his themes, his methods, and his place in the scheme of things.

Now accountably out of print, *Blindness* (1926) is an astonishingly artful first novel to have been written by a twenty-year-old Oxford undergraduate. Ostensibly another example of the familiar novel of initiation, in which a sensitive young man is confronted and dislocated by external reality in the form of personal tragedy, Green's first effort contains subtleties and ironies which set it apart.

The book is organized in three sections: Caterpillar, Chrysalis, and Butterfly, and although this overtly symbolic nomenclature suggests the central theme of growth, it does not adequately reflect the complexities of the process.

The first section is in the form of diary entries. John Haye, a schoolboy at Noat, conceives of the diary as "a sort of pipe to draw off the swamp water." Intellectually precocious, he has tastes that are, for the most part, centered on literature and art. The entries serve much the same purpose as those of Stephen Dedalus's diary in the closing pages of *A Portrait of the Artist:* to adumbrate a developing esthetic consciousness, to accentuate the isolation of the boy, and to afford opportunity for first efforts at recording and evaluating experience and impression.

The picture of John himself emerges by indirection through the medium of these entries. We glimpse a lonely, sensitive, perceptive, and somewhat defensive young man, whose literary tastes are oddly advanced. He admires polished or pungent letter writers, ranging from Carlyle through the Brontës to Van Gogh. His preferences include, as prose stylists, Lytton Strachey, Anatole France, Gogol, George Moore, Dostoievsky, and Turgeniev, all of whom he seems to have read with understanding.

Clearly he is set apart by his classmates, and he masks whatever may be his real reaction by referring to the social ostracism he experiences as "incredibly funny." Occasionally he senses the basis for it ("What an odious superior fellow I am now!"), but for the most part he holds himself aloof and immerses himself in his inner life of literature and art. His desire

[5]

to write increases, and he begins to sound more and more like the arrogant young Dedalus: "At dinner tonight Mamma informed me in one of her rare pronouncements on myself, that I always kept people at arm's length. It sounds an awful thing to write, but I seldom meet anyone who interests me more than myself: my own fault, I suppose."

Tragedy now strikes abruptly. In a fragment of a letter from one classmate to another, we learn that John has been blinded. While he was traveling home on the train, his face has been cut and his eyes destroyed by the shattered glass of the window, broken by a large stone thrown by a boy. This gratuitous calamity, reducing his diary entries, his esthetic interests, and his arrogance to meaningless, comes with apparently no warning. Yet Green has furnished several veiled portents of the event. John's classmates throwing stones at his window anticipate the later destructive act of the small boy, and together with references to spots before his eyes and being so tired he could "hardly see at all," reverberate in retrospect, suggesting a spiritual affliction which antedates the physical.

In Part II, Chrysalis, the boy, now at Barwood, the family home in the country, gropes in despair in his cocoon of blindness. His stepmother, a horsey, self-centered and insensitive, but somehow pathetic woman, fumbles fitfully toward communication with John, but the bridges between them are few and shaky. His isolation is terribly absolute, and he is imprisoned in a circle of emptiness, surrounded by objects and people outside his grasp. The resulting impersonality of his new world is aptly prefigured by a chapter heading: "Her, Him, Them."

The focus now shifts abruptly as we meet Joan Entwhistle and her gin-soaked father, a disenfranchised parson living in a dilapidated cottage near Barwood. Joan accepts her situation with a kind of slovenly stoicism ("But what was the good of keeping clean now?"), and it is not clear whether she sees no possibility of escape or wishes none. Her occasional erotic fantasies seem to leave her unmoved, and she cares for her father's and her needs with tinned food, greasy dishwater, and an unkempt house.

John and Joan, whom he persists in calling June, meet and begin to walk together. There is a kind of fencing playfulness in their relationship which masks a wistful reaching toward each other. In the end, however, the disapproval of John's stepmother, his awareness of Joan's limitations, and her own apathy, which binds her to her father, combine to damp off the relationship, and it comes to nothing.

The final sequence of events and adjustments begins when Mrs. Haye pulls up her roots at Barwood and takes John to London. Initially depressed by the strangeness of his surroundings, he confronts his blindness and accepts it, sensing a new beginning for himself in the city. His other senses are more acute now to compensate for his sightlessness. Yet he feels ill, feverish. Abruptly, he experiences a kind of wild rising joy, then collapse. We finally learn, from his later letter to a former classmate, that he has had a fit of some sort, possibly hereditary epilepsy, but that he has recovered and is happy to be alive. The letter and the book end with a question: "Why am I so happy today?"

That the plot is slight and not the center of things is clear by this recital of it. Nor is this simply another novel of isolation and spiritual desolation not uncommon in the mid 1920s, although it is of course that. Clearly John is cast into the wasteland, and the novel in a sense is the story of his attempt to find the river of life again, or possibly for the first time. In existentialist terms, the novel portrays the self confronting the absurd and the contingent here combined into the sense-lessly destructive act of Haye's blinding, and coming to terms with them.

What seems most central, however, is the organic cohesive-ness achieved by Green's technique. What looks at first to be a rather disjointed novel turns out to be, when viewed more closely, almost a tissue of connectives. Nearly everything, we realize, is connected with nearly everything else. John's catastrophe, for example, is, as we have seen, prefigured by his stone-throwing classmates, whom he ironically refers to as blind. After his tragedy, he is linked with Joan by the scars on both their faces, hers also the result of being cut by broken glass, a bottle hurled by her drunken father. John's sightlessness also connects itself with the blindness of the old dog Ruffles, whom his stepmother thinks possibly should be destroyed and put out of his misery, and with the newborn kittens, whom she thinks should be drowned immediately. Finally, his relationship with Joan, blindly opposed by Mrs. Haye, also causes his Nanny to observe, disapprovingly, that young people always go into those things blind.

Perhaps the principal connective, however, is water. The purpose of John's diary, we recall, was to draw off the swamp water. Two of his classmates have a waterfight in his room. Rain spoils the summer camp. John's favorite and only out-door recreation is fishing, and at one point he speculates on his fondness for the river: What is it, he wonders, that is so attractive about the sound of disturbed water? "The contrast of sound to appearance, perhaps. Water looks so like a varnished surface that to see it break up, move and sound in moving is infinitely pleasing. Also it is exhilarating to see an unfortunate upset." Ironically, it is he who is the unfortunate soon to be upset in the flux.

It is raining when we first see John after the accident, mingling Nanny's tears of compassion. Rain interrupts Joan's recollection of Mrs. Haye and, later, presages the meeting of John and Joan. The rain passes away as their relationship dissipates and dies, and the final rain brings with it another change—the departure for London. There the sun shines as the new life begins.

We diminish the cryptic richness of this structural device if we press for exact meaning. Let us say rather that water seems to be the enveloping medium, amniotic perhaps, which binds together all the characters, and from which John emerges at the end in a kind of rebirth.

If some parts of the novel are inexplicable, their interacting net effect seems clear. In the book, method and message merge: blindness, like death in Joyce's short story, "The Dead," is universal. Mrs. Haye's insensitivity blinds her to the extent of John's anguish. Joan is blind to her slovenliness and the extent of her emotional impoverishment and entrapment. Her father is blind to his selfishness. Perhaps, ironically, it is only John who ultimately emerges from the blindness of his early dilettantish arrogance and sense of self to a large vision of humble acceptance, to spiritual sight.

This brings us to the ending of the novel, and to Green's crowning ambiguity. If we are to take John's final letter at face value, he has emerged completely from the blackness of despair. "I am so happy to be in the centre of things again, and to be alive," he writes. Yet at this point we recall his now almost desperate resolve to carry forward his writing ("What was the use of his going blind if he did not write?"), his sense that Barwood, representing the past, must be laughing at him because by going away he had found out how helpless he was, and finally, his resolution not to be laughed at by his classmates. He would not "let them see him crushed under his blindness, they would despise him for it. He must first make out how he stood with life in general so that he could show them how much better off he was than they." We are left wondering if his happiness is genuine, or if he is simply putting up a good front, or if, as seems more likely, it is a little of each, combining into a viable persona for the young writer. In any case, we are left contemplating a kind of enigma Conrad would have understood and approved. In this unusually deft and advanced first novel, then, Green was able to lay hands on the kind of method he would continue to employ and develop throughout his subsequent work.

At first glance, his second novel, *Living* (1929), a considerably more externalized work, would seem to have no connection with his first, but as we shall see, there are important connectives. Completely shifting locale and subject, from public school to iron foundry, from young intellectual to foundry workers, Green derives his new material from his own experiences when, on leaving Oxford, he went to work in the family business, a corporation he was later to manage until he retired and left the directorial reins in the hands of his son. However different the material, the young novelist's concern with technique remains and grows.

Condensing the scenic method of the first novel, in *Living* he deals for the most part in short, disparate, fragmented, and rapidly shifting scenes which reveal the drab lives and involvements of the Birmingham foundry workers. The disjointed narrative thus established effectively mirrors the lack of wholeness or completeness in their lives. We see them at work, and learn of the enmity between them and the works manager, Bridges, who is known to the men as 'Tis 'im, a harried supervisor continually frustrated in his attempts to maintain production. We meet the principal characters. Craigan, the taciturn, aging moulder, rules his domicile with a firm hand, listens to the wireless, and reads Dickens. Joe Gates, the blustering, self-pitying father of Lily, who keeps house, and the young Jim Dale, Craigan's helper, comprise the household. It is a life of drab routine and ever-increasing entrapment for Lily. She stirs restlessly toward escape and fulfillment, although she would have trouble defining either. She wants to get a job, but Craigan won't allow it. Originally Dale's girl, she shifts her affections to Bert Jones, a young blade at the foundry who is also dissatisfied with his lot, and who mutters occasionally his intention to leave for "Orstrylia" to make his fortune.

Young Richard Dupret, son of the dying foundry owner, strikes an incongruous note as he tries ineffectually to impose his will on his subordinates. He emerges as a rather shallow, languid, narcissistic, and esthetically oriented young man whose comments on the beautiful face of one of the young workman and whose meditations on the beauty of shape of the iron castings place him at odds with his surroundings.

Another incongruity of a more affirmative sort is Mrs. Eames, who lives next door to the Craigan household. She is earthy, fertile, and fulfilled—accepting and contented with her situation, her husband, and her babies. A kind of life force, she stands in positive contrast to the death-like greyness of the town and its inhabitants.

The petty foundry rivalries and intrigues serve as a backdrop against which the basic conflict of the novel emerges. Craigan, fearful that Lily will marry Bert and move out, leaving him alone in his old age, opposes the relationship, seeking to interest her in Dale instead. But Lily has made up her mind,

[11]

and stands firm against Craigan's taciturn opposition, Dale's sullen overtures, and her father's bluster, threats, and blows. Bert Jones means freedom to Lily—at least so she thinks, and she will not relinquish him. Her sense of purpose in the relationship exceeds his own, and as her desire to make definite plans increases, so does his uneasiness.

Meanwhile, Dupret's father sinks further toward death. Not even the bewildered prostitute hired by Mrs. Dupret can regenerate him. Richard Dupret continues to be generally ineffectual at the foundry, which seems to have, bafflingly to him, a life of its own. When his father dies he does finally manage to assert himself by ordering the older men at the foundry laid off, including Craigan and Lily's father, who promptly manages to get himself arrested for cursing in public. Events now accelerate. Dale decides to move out. Lily and Bert elope.

But the flight seems doomed from the outset. He brings to her, at the train, a bouquet of tulips from the cemetery, which render futile her embarrassed attempts to remain inconspicuous, and serve as a sinister harbinger of the fate of their union. The plan is to lodge Lily with Bert's parents in Liverpool until details of the marriage and passage out of the country, now to Canada, can be arranged. But Bert's parents have moved from their shop, and the dreary night-time search for their new address through increasingly deteriorated areas of the city plods dreadeningly on. Finally, in a superbly evoked setting of waterfront squalor, they come to a dead end. Lily weeps quietly as Bert leads her to a tram stop, thrusts her bag into her hands, and bolts.

Back at home with Craigan, she recuperates from her ordeal. Dale won't come back, so the household of three carries on. At the end of the novel, Lily visits the new Eames baby next door. Life, or rather living, goes on.

As in *Blindness*, plot does not seem to be Green's chief concern. A kind of self-conscious experimentalism is at work, chiefly evidenced in the narrative passages. By dislocating syntax, by compressing and eliminating articles, and by dealing in indirect discourse, Green achieves a colloquially crabbed ungainliness which epitomizes the lives of the workers, as when Bert Jones speaks to one of his mates: "Mr. Jones said what was the time. Mr. Smith went out to where by bending down he could see clock on the wall in shop next to them." Or: "Evening. Was spring. Heavy blue clouds stayed over above. In small back garden of villa small tree was with yellow buds. On table in back room daffodils, faded, were between ferns in a vase."

Difficult to convey by these brief passages, the technique is, for the most part, effective, although occasionally self-conscious and obtrusive, much like an overly loud musical background to a motion picture. There is nothing obtrusive, however, about Green's dialogue, which carries a far heavier burden in *Living* than in *Blindness*. His sense of the idiom of the workers seems unerring and deft, and the rough, terse rhythms of their speech portray the incompletion and anti-romantic quality of their lives more effectively than do Green's attempts to mirror these things by narrative techniques.

Overriding such matters as plot, characterization, dialogue, narrative technique, and brilliance of individual scenes, however, is what seems to be the most significant aspect of the novel, as it was also of *Blindness*: connectedness. There is an only slightly veiled relationship implicit when young Dupret comments at the beginning of the book about the beautiful face of Jim Dale. Both suddenly seem incongruous in their surroundings. Both are destined to be jilted by their respective young ladies.

But there are subtler connectives: birds. In this novel Green develops pervasively but elusively a correspondence between natural object and human event and attitude. The natural object is the bird. Ranging from a fairly overt significance as symbols of flight in the early passages, so that Gates' childish paper airplanes are seen as feeble and somewhat pathetic imitations, birds function in a variety of ways in the novel, not always in a clearly defined fashion, to be sure. As a matter of fact, the central significance of these symbols always seems to be at least partially masked, as in the case of Wallace Stevens' blackbirds, which can be looked at thirteen ways and more, and the reader, viewing the variety of contexts in which birds appear in *Living*, feels many of them fluttering elusively through his fingers.

Some specific usages are of course clear enough. Old Tupe in the foundry tells Bert to fly high and take his pick of the tarts circling up to him like birds. Racing pigeons kept by a man next door to the Craigan household emphasize by contrast the lifelessness of the menage. A sparrow caught in their window reveals their ineptness and approximates their own entrapment. They are all too clumsy to free it, but Mrs. Eames is able to. Birds figure from time to time in rather elaborate Homeric similes in which they serve as analogues for obscure states of feeling.

Pigeons are conspicuous in the novel, hovering over Lily as she herself prepares to fly the coop with Bert, flocking around her as do her scattered thoughts when the day of flight approaches, and homing as her thoughts always return to her future with Bert. After her dejected return, her connection with the birds becomes overt as her father comments that she's not eating enough to keep a pigeon alive. At the end of the novel, pigeons fill the air over Birmingham, and as Lily watches them she hears the cry of the new Eames baby. As the pigeons soar, her own feelings "make expeditions away from herself," as she begins to recover from her experience with Bert. She begins to feel the possibility of a new beginning for her, and as if to celebrate and confirm this sense of renewal, she visits the new Eames baby, while pigeons gather in what seems at once benediction and augury.

This use of birds becomes a kind of shorthand by which Green provides vague portents of unarticulated feeling. They seem to function as objective correlatives, except that it is not at all clear what they correlate. Somewhat as was the case with the water images in *Blindness*, they serve to bind the book together, connecting its characters, and somehow non-discursively making a pervasive reality of the title.

"Fog was so dense, bird that had been disturbed went flat into a balustrade and slowly fell, dead, at her feet." These opening lines of *Party Going* (1938) seem initially to be but a continuation of the terse syntax of *Living*. Quickly, however, the style lengthens out, and we see that the condensation of the opening serves mainly to register upon us the impact of the death of that central bird. It is the abruptly dissonant initial chord in a prose fugue.

Ostensibly, *Party Going* concerns a group of upper-middle-class idlers whose plans for a trek to the south of France are frustrated by a pea-soup fog which paralyzes all the trains and leaves everyone stranded at a London station. Killing time with tea, whisky, gossip, and endless much ados about elusive nothings in the station hotel, they wait out the fog and resume their plans as it finally lifts. At the end of this novel about a lull in these lives, the reader is left wondering which was the lull, the wait in the station or their regular round. "But surely that's just it," one of the characters observes two thirds of the way through the book, "there's nothing to do." One feels with these people there never is.

In a sense a novel of the absurd, the book centers on a joke, a running gag about a character named Embassy Richard, who surprisingly turns up at the end to join the party. Richard, inordinately fond of parties and receptions, has acquired his sobriquet because of his invariable presence on the guest list at embassy receptions. The story is that he published, on the social page, his regrets at not attending a reception to which, as the appropriate ambassador pointed out publicly, he'd not been invited in the first place. Speculation as to the amount of his embarrassment, whether or not he'd been framed, and who really did what to whom and why, serve as a connective or motif throughout the novel. Nobody, it seems, has the straight of it, and the tedious reiteration of the story not only suggests the tedium of lives in which there is very little else to talk about, but is also a reflection of the pervasive cosmic uncertainty in the novel. What is clear is that Embassy Richard, who occupies, perhaps by default, so much of the attention of those who merely stand and wait, is spiritually one of them, as attested to by the ease and nonchalance with which he postpones his own plans, if any, to join the party at the end.

And why not? Richard's superficiality fits in perfectly with that of the group. Selfish, shallow, each is concerned primarily with his own equilibrium, for, fog or clear, there is really nowhere for any of them to go. In this devastatingly reductive novel, even the initial compassion shown by the outsider Miss Fellowes (is she all fellows?) toward the dead pigeon quickly assumes a macabre quality. In a surrealistic scene she washes the bird in the ladies' room, and then, as the macabre farce deepens, she bundles it neatly into a paper parcel, gives it to a young man to throw away, then finally retrieves it.

That the dead bird is central to the story is clear, even if its significance is not. Somehow the pigeon and Miss Fellowes are connected, for after ceremoniously scrubbing it she feels ill and wonders whether she'll fall downstairs, like the bird. Momentarily, after palming off the parcel on the young man, she feels better, suggesting a similarity between pigeon and albatross, but then, obscurely compelled, she reclaims her talisman.

Another binding agent is the fog which surrounds the station, blurring, distorting, and ultimately leveling everything. Perhaps it is like Forster's Marabar caves, a kind of reality which swallows and dwarfs the little people who scurry through it; it may also serve as the shadow which frustrates and limits all in Eliot's world of hollow men. It recognizes no caste; Miss Wray groping her way to the station might be a typist, a poisoner, anything. Superbly described by Green, it transforms familiar prosaic London into a surrealist montage of wet leaves, blurred headlights, disturbed birds, horns, shimmering policemen dressed in rubber, and swirling blankets of mist. "One moment you were in dirty cotton wool saturated with iced water and then out of it into ravines of cold sweating granite with cave-dwellers' windows and entrances."

The group's reaction to the fog roughly mirrors its reaction to any other kind of reality. Miss Wray feels powerless because she forgot to bring her "charms," a wooden pistol, an egg with tiny elephants in it, a painted top, on all of which she apparently depends to bring some sort of magic into her dreary social round. Amabel, the shallow and completely self-centered beauty, wants to get out of "this frightful fog" as she wants to avoid everything else that in any way takes her out of the spotlight. She wonders if anyone is "really doing anything about it." Max, the playboy host of the group, does what he can about it, which in the main consists of ordering extra rooms, drinks, and food.

The dead bird increases its hold on the book. Suggestions of death become more overt as the crowd in the station increases. Julia, surveying the station with growing horror, "thought it was like an enormous doctor's waiting room and that it would be like that when they were all dead and waiting at the gates." Now the shutters are closed over the entrances to prevent any more crowding, and this, in effect, entombs the group. Miss Fellows, in the meantime, needing a stimulant, has a stiff drink, which lays her out. Her tormented visions are of death.

Even in the presence of this final leveler, however, caste is still operative. The group, fittingly enough, look down from their hotel windows upon the milling throng which Green, in a series of metaphysical conceits, shows us to have Protean propensities. Julia, watching the smoke rising from countless cigarettes, thinks of "November sun striking through mist rising off water." The movement of small groups is like corpuscles moving through veins. Characteristically, her governing vision is that of a queen on a balcony viewing her subjects. Later, she is terrified by the mass and closes the window. After all, she tells Max, "one must not hear too many cries for help in this world." One would have nothing left. The crowd is obliterated by her act and her words. "It was extraordinary how quiet their room became once that window was shut." She opens it again as the crowd begins to sing, and sees the thousands of people "woven tight as any office carpet." She imagines them "like sheep with golden tenor voices" who are "happily singing their troubles away and being good companions." In fact, as Green tells us, they are Welshmen up to London for a match, and they are singing in Welsh about the rape of a silly girl on a mountain in Wales. Julia's misapprehensions seem representative of the group's insulation from reality.

The crowd takes on more sinister overtones. The continual dull roar bears down on the group inside "like clouds upon a mountain so they were obscured and levelled and, as though they had been airmen, in danger of running fatally into earth." The roar now sounds like "numbers of aeroplanes flying by." The culminating image is inevitable. "What targets," says a man surveying the crowd, "what targets for a bomb." Fittingly, in our final glimpse the crowd is "like ruins in the wet."

In the midst of this paralysis, emptiness, and death, the desultory fidgeting of the group is broken only by the speculation about Embassy Richard, which is one kind of subplot, and the tussle of Amabel and Julia over Max, which is another. The relationship between Max and Amabel is abrasive but neither can abandon it. Max's flirtation with Julia has about as much chance of surviving Amabel's foray into the group to retrap her elusive man as a snowball in the furious hell of a woman scorned.

The duel Max and Amabel fight is quiet but grim. She must have control of him, and he must not allow it. Alternately he buckles and bolts, but in the end the duel turns out to be but one more empty ritual in their lives. They patch things up and will remain together simply because they belong together; there is nowhere else for either of them to go,

[19]

nothing else for either of them to do. Amabel settles for the illusion of love; Max settles for Amabel. The one unpredictable note in the outcome is the revelation that Amabel has been seeing the ubiquitous Embassy Richard.

The topical significance of Green's fable, for it is that in part, cannot be ignored. These sterile people enmeshed in vacuity are fitting bomb targets indeed, for the year is 1939, and Green's revelations of the decayed state of upper-middle-class English society make Armageddon somehow fitting. But the novel cannot be seen as simply or even mainly topical. It has to do with nothingness and the absurd, and the pathetic attempts of the hollow men and women to countervail the emptiness. Such themes are not confinable to the year of a war; such comment is not simply social criticism. Before it became fashionable to do so in England, Green wrote an existentialist novel.

The dutiful and industrious reader, attempting to move methodically through Green's canon in chronological order only to find himself adrift in progressively widening circles of bewilderment, tends now to sigh with relief as Green at this point calls time out with *Pack My Bag* (1940), an autobiographical account of the years from childhood through Oxford. Written during the years 1938–1939, the book is permeated with and indeed instigated by premonitions of death in the impending war. He tells us he wants to "put down what comes to mind before one is killed." What comes to mind, it turns out, is a rather familiar and representative assortment of childhood and schoolboy experiences, again suggesting that to Green, plot, or at least novelty, is not the most important element. What brings fresh meaning to his narrative is the wry humor with which he recalls his youth.

[20]

His achievement of droll honesty ("I was born a mouth breather with a silver spoon"), involving both self-derision and self-acceptance, must not have come easily, for one theme of the book is shyness, a characteristic of Green himself and one which he tells us he would like to see more of in human relationships. In an age in which great emphasis and considerable earnestness have been lavished upon "communication" in human relationships, Green's tack takes us into a refreshing breeze which rocks the boat, at one end of which perches Lawrence, at the other, assorted social psychologists. But Green is by no means a novice at or naive with respect to human relationships. Initially bluff on the subject ("Most things boil down to people"), he proves to be astonishingly deft in his analysis of a wide range of relationships, and shyness in his sense proves to involve gentleness and a need of mystery rather than bumbling awkwardness.

The honesty with which he remembers and retells is nowhere more apparent than in his speculation as to whether boys assume grief in crises because it is expected of them. The case in point is a severe injury to his parents in Mexico, and the news that they are not expected to live. "I began to dramatize the shock I knew I had had," he tells us, "into what I thought it ought to feel like." In other words, he puts on a face to meet the faces that he meets. During the chapel service, he stages a dumb show of anguish for the benefit of the headmaster's wife, simultaneously condemning himself for it. He lets himself go, willing himself "to imagine the parents writhing in agony, pulled faces, showed all the agitation I could and at the same time, there can be no excuse, watched her to see that she got the full force of it." Through all this pretense there moves the dull knife of genuine grief, and the boy's bewilderment about the true state of his feelings, together with his horror at his sorry mime, reveals not only Green's painful honesty but his acuity at probing complex states of feeling and his deftness at exposing them, both of which abilities are abundantly present in his novels.

Pack My Bag reveals several correspondences between the young Green and John Haye, central character of *Blindness*. Green, like his fictional surrogate, helped organize an Arts Society in school and served as its secretary. The group apparently included most of the anti-games and mildly anti-establishment esthetes in the school. Green, like Haye, was interested in writing and started his novel about Haye while still in school. Unlike Haye, he made it to Oxford for one year, during which he was apparently rarely sober. The inebriation was not always and entirely produced by alcohol, however. The first-year students were discovering the world of ideas and of compatibly sufficient leisure. Green found the mixture perhaps overly congenial, for guilt apparently set in, and he went down at the end of the year to see how the "other half" lived, driven by what he calls his complex to go to work in a factory with his "wet podgy hands."

Near the end of *Pack My Bag* Green alludes briefly to his work. "I write books," he tells us simply, "but I am not proud of this any more than anyone is of their nails growing." Having entered this disclaimer, he disappears behind the mask of his subsequent fiction, perhaps, like Joyce's artist, paring those growing nails, but not, I think, indifferently.

With *Caught* (1943), we learn that Green's premonition of death in war was, at least for him, fortunately inaccurate. But the subject of the book is war, and death is no stranger. The novel is about the Auxiliary Fire Service (in which Green himself served) before and, briefly, during the blitz.

Green tells us that his characters, "while founded on the reality of that time," are imaginary. "In this book only 1940 in London is real. It is the effect of that time that I have written into the fiction of *Caught*." Not surprisingly, he has written into it a great deal besides.

Again, plot may be rather simply stated. Richard Roe, a widower, joins the Fire Service as an Auxiliary, having sent his five-year-old son Christopher down to the country for safety. Christopher is staying at the family place with Dy, Roe's dead wife's sister, having weathered a brief and harmless kidnapping by the deranged sister of Pye, a member of the regular Fire Service. The boy is drawn with considerable economy of characterization: "Christopher was like any other child of his age, not very interested or interesting, strident with health. He enjoyed teasing and was careful no-one should know what he felt." Richard and some of the other central characters are also quickly sketched rather than developed in detail. Interestingly enough, it is the subordinate characters who seem most fully developed. The overage Piper, of the ingratiating manners and rank odor, earning our disgust currying favor and our pity because of "Mother," his irascible old whiner of a wife, is an example. Pye himself, a petty tyrant of a careerist, alternately bullying and fawning, his chief objective apparently keeping his record clear and future pension thus intact, is splendidly portrayed. A central achievement of Green in this novel is the manner in which Pye rises to an almost tragic grandeur as he discovers he may have committed incest with his own sister in the dark years before (we are never completely certain), and if so may be responsible for her derangement.

Hilly, one of the Women's Auxiliaries, is somewhat more shadowy, possibly because of her more direct involvement with Roe, the central shadow. Bovine and of limited aspiration, she meets his physical need when he is able to free himself sufficiently from the specter of his dead wife to manifest a need. Dy, called Mum by Christopher but not wife by Roe, inheriting the thorns without the roses, exists in quiet frustration and blurred outline.

If the center seems in shadow while the surroundings are illuminated, we must remember Green's announced objective: to evoke the London of 1940. His strokes here are sure. He captures for us the pre-blitz boredom and self-consciousness of men in uniform, men feeling like parasites, botching their first missions, enduring the daily round of petty routine and discipline ("We come here ready for at least death, and then we get into trouble for not doing under our beds."). We sense also the mood of abandonment, the compulsive love-making rituals of martyred leavetaking, each farewell a rationale for further promiscuity.

And then, the searing purgative of the blitz, and the reduction of life to bare essentials. Uniforms are now worn without thought. Fire are fought through the blazing nights until men are killed or nerves give way. Green achieves, in this evocation, a remarkable presence, and he does so chiefly through his felicitious rendering of working-class speech. Green's own work in the foundry and his earlier *Living* had provided the apprenticeship for this, but now the dialogue has become less stylized, more natural.

Characteristically, Green's title pervades his book. Not only is London of 1940 "caught" for us, but all of the characters are too. The mood is one of suspension in emptiness; arrest, transfixion. Actions are inconclusive, and the paralysis of the characters is expressed in a manner not completely dissimilar to that of Joyce's *Dubliners*.

The central characters are also individually caught, each in his own way. Pye, caught by his past, is eventually destroyed by it as his guilt at the realization of his probable incest drives him ultimately to suicide. Roe is also the victim of his past. His dead wife's hold on him is tenacious and crippling. He is ghosted by her, and only at the end, as he compulsively recalls the fire raids to Dy, does he exorcise the past sufficiently to become uncaught, if not completely free.

If there is some hope in his final situation, it is the son Christopher who is even more the chief symbol of hope. Although Roe seems partially extricated from his bonds at the end, Christopher has come through his early abduction and the war thus far unscathed and sound. At the end Roe and he are together. Roe is at least partially purged; Christopher has nothing to purge. Only in retrospect does Green's subtle skill in suggesting Roe's partial liberation from the past become apparent. At the beginning of the book, when he visits Christopher at the family house, the gardens and countryside are so described as to have a kind of luminosity which is hypnotic in effect and probably indicative of the hold the place has on Roe because of his dead wife. At the end, however, scant attention is paid to surroundings, as Richard relives and thus releases his recent trauma. Setting is not so dominant now, because he is working free of it. He is, then, able to turn on Dy, who refuses to forgive the dead Pye and his demented sister. "All you bloody women with all your talk," he snaps, and we sense that he is also turning on, or rather away from, his dead wife. As he realizes, "he had got away at last." He even dismisses Christopher, but only until after tea. A minor victory, perhaps, but his own.

Green, in *Caught*, extends his use of the scenic method.

Much of the book is montage, an intricate network of short simultaneous scenes connected by image, instant, or innuendo. And the central innuendo is that although all are somehow initially caught, there exists at least the possibility of movement from bondage toward freedom, from isolation toward love.

This is the central theme of Green's best-known novel, *Loving* (1945). The title of the book is its subject. Using as microcosm the almost completely isolated world of a household of British servants in an Irish manor during World War II, Green shows us all the kinds of loving: domestic and foreign, innocent and adulterous, maternal and oedipal, requited and unrequited, heterosexual and, at least latently, homosexual, tender and grotesque, comic and serious. In retrospect all the forms tend to merge, and this may be the triumph of the book, for the tension throughout the novel has been that of love versus loneliness, and it is love, or rather loving, that wins out in the end.

To be sure, Green's tone is in part ironic, and alerted to the quality of fable or fairy tale by the opening words, "Once upon a day," we find confirmation at the end, when we learn that the two central characters "were married and lived happily ever after." Yet in spite of that distancing device, and despite the comic perspective which he maintains, this is Green's most affirmative work thus far. In a sense, it is the answer to *Party Going*. Both novels are existentialist. Set differently, both nonetheless reveal the absurd world and the void. The central difference between them is that in the early novel the desultory attempts of the partygoers to fill the void are ultimately futile, while in the later one at least some of the characters manage to fill the void by loving.

Many of the attempts are fumbling and incomplete, for communication is difficult. The book is peppered with conversations at cross-purposes, and misunderstandings abound, as when Raunce mistakes an insurance investigator for an agent of the dread I.R.A. But connection is worth all, and in the end it is achieved. Eldon, the butler whose death opens the novel, calls out in vain to "Ellen" as he dies. Raunce, his successor, contemplating his beloved Edie at the end, utters her name softly, and the cycle is complete. Death yields to renewal, isolation to connection.

Everybody loves somebody. Eldon loves Ellen. Miss Burch, the unfulfilled housekeeper, loves Eldon. Edith and Kate, the two maids, love each other with a kind of nascent but passive lesbian attachment. Kate also loves Paddy, the grotesque lampman. Mrs. Welch, the cook, loves her obnoxious grandson Albert. Larger Albert, Raunce's helper, loves Edith. Mrs. Tennant, the owner of the house, loves everything just the way it is. Her daughter-in-law loves Dermot, an Irishman, not her husband. Raunce loves his mother, his Albert, and his Edith.

It is the effect of the loving on the lovers that makes and resolves the novel, and the most remarkable transformation is that of Raunce. Indeed, our change of mind about this comic hero is one of Green's central achievements in the novel. We are initially repelled by his crass connivery and his self-centered petty mindedness. We are amused by his regressive attachment to Mummy in England. He writes solicitous letters to her and promptly lays his head on his arms and goes off to sleep. He is not a pretty fellow, but he gradually becomes one. We come to be touched by his initially gauche fumblings toward love. He fails as cavalier or Casanova, and instead it is ultimately a restrained gentleness toward Edith which comes to the surface. With love comes responsibility, and with responsibility guilt over the war. When Albert enlists, the guilt bears in and helps promote Raunce's return to England. And although he does return to Mummy's land in the end, it is as a man with a wife.

The consequences of loving are no less apparent with Kate and Paddy. Significantly, no one else in the novel can understand a word he says, but Kate has no difficulty, and the communication between the two seems to answer the needs of both. Kate is liberated from her attachment to Edith, and sees her relationship to Paddy as a natural and inevitable filling of the void ("Well there's not much else to think of is there Edie?"), and accepts it simply as "the way things are."

But loving is not simply roses without thorns, and it is Violet Tennant who is lacerated. Her husband at war, her mother-in-law away, she is discovered by the maid in bed with her Irish lover. Torn by guilt and fear of exposure, and by the claims on her heart of her husband and his mother, she ultimately renounces her lover. In an ambiguous moment when we see Mrs. Tennant's sudden grim smile at her daughter-in-law's back, we wonder if she has known about the affair all along.

As in *Party Going*, a dead bird figures significantly. Peacock rather than pigeon, it is choked to death by Mrs. Welch's grandson, Albert. As death yields to renewal at the end the dead peacock is obliterated by live ones fed by Edith and by doves fluttering around her in a kind of benedictory vision, as in *Living*. It is an epiphany of fulfillment to Raunce, not only emotional but esthetic: "What he saw then he watched so that it could be guessed that he was in pain with his great delight. For what with the peacocks bowing at her purple skirts, the white doves nodding on her shoulders round her brilliant cheeks and her great eyes that blinked tears of happiness, it made a picture." The understatement of the last phrase is more a matter of Raunce's limited vocabulary than of the impact of all this upon him, for it is only then that Raunce can speak her name softly, and in so doing fill the void left by the empty cry of the dying butler at the beginning. The void has been filled, perhaps not by love but at least by loving.

The void returns in *Back* (1946). As in *Caught*, the central character is haunted by a dead woman; in this case it is Charley Summers' late mistress, Rose. Indeed, a central subject of the novel is not only Rose but roses; they are everywhere. Initially conspiring to haunt him, in the end they confirm and celebrate his renewal and release from the past. *Back* may be Green's *Four Quartets*.

Back from the war, a repatriated prisoner suffering from combat fatigue and consequent loss of nerve, Charley visits Rose's grave and is surrounded, under trees of mourning, by "rose after rose after rose." Roses had been his downfall in the war; he hadn't noticed the sniper's gun under the rose bush, and it had cost him his leg. Crippled by that and by his maiming love, his pilgrimage is regressive; his encounters with the past are unsatisfactory and painful. James, Rose's husband, is banal; Ridley, the child who may or may not have been sired by Charley, is indifferent. Rose's mother is deranged, mistaking Charley for her long-dead brother. These are not healing confrontations, and only add to his pain. He has more problems than prospects.

His central problem becomes that of distinguishing the real from the unreal, for one of the most notable aspects of the novel is its hallucinatory quality. Rose's father introduces Charley to Nancy Whittmore, Rose's half-sister, and Charley is immediately and obsessively certain that she is Rose and that the whole story of her death has been trumped up.

It is this obsession that almost unhinges his mind, and the central action of the novel is his agonizingly slow and fumbling struggle back through hallucination to reality is an eerie farce not only of mistaken identity but coincidence. Almost everyone in the story, it turns out, knows everyone else, and there is always an undercurrent of mystery in each relationship which evokes an aura of nightmare.

His own initial relationship with Nancy seems doomed: he thinks her Rose, she thinks him mad. Like everything else about his life, this is sure to lead nowhere, for nothing he does is right. Even the filing system he develops at the office breaks down, as do his fumblings toward a relationship with his secretary. In one of the several ironies of the novel, it is her perfidy which helps him around the corner toward life again. Having taken her to James's house for the weekend, he discovers she's found her way to her host's bed. Only mildly upset, he finds himself, however, suddenly and freshly conscious of his own needs, and thus finds himself with Nancy again, now increasingly aware that she is not Rose.

The second major irony resolves the novel. Mr. Grant's terminal illness brings Mrs. Grant to her senses, and brings new life to Charley. Victim of a stroke, the old man lies helpless. Mrs. Grant in her new clarity tries to cope but needs help, so Nancy moves in and, to all intents and purposes, takes the place of Rose. Mrs. Grant accepts her husband's illegitimate daughter as her own, and when, in response to her need for a man in the house, Charley moves in, the family is united.

Mr. Grant dies, his job done. It was he who had paved the way for the plot by siring both Rose and Nancy, then precipitated it by introducing Charley to Nancy. It is he who, happily married all these years to Mrs. Grant, serves as an example of successful second love. Now he withdraws, leaving the stage and the future to Charley.

A bravura scene ends the book. Charley has proposed and has been accepted; Nancy's only condition is that there be a "trial trip." He goes to her room, where she awaits him, naked on the bed. He kneels beside her, overwhelmed. The pink shade of the lit lamp "spills a light of roses over her," roses of all colors, covering her hands, legs, stomach, breasts, neck: "She had shut her eyes to let him have his fill, but it was too much, for he burst into tears again, he buried his face in her side just below the ribs, and bawled like a child. 'Rose,' he called out, not knowing he did so, 'Rose.' 'There,' Nancy said, 'there,' pressed his head with her hands. His tears wetted her. The salt water ran down between her legs. And she knew what she had taken on. It was no more or less, really, than she had expected."

The only unambiguous thing about this scene is its ambiguity. Is this the ultimate regression for Charley, his final hallucination? Has the rosy glow broken him down, so that the dead Rose finally claims him? Certainly it is possible to interpret the scene thus, and there is a strain of rather contrived religious symbolism in the novel which tends to support such a reading. We are told early on that Charley will deny Rose thrice. Later, struggling for separation from her hold on him, he speaks of her "as of a rib that had been removed." By now burying his head below Nancy's rib and calling her Rose, does he want his own back? And has he only tears to offer Nancy? Sterile seed indeed: no crops grow in salted soil.

Yet another view of all this is possible, in many senses a

rosier view. By embracing Nancy and unconsciously calling out "Rose," Charley may be marrying past and present, and in so doing, exorcising the ghost and burying the dead past in the living warm present of Nancy's arms. As in *Loving*, we may now have come full circle, death yielding to renewal once more. It may even be that for Charley, this beatific vision of Nancy bathed in roses represents not regression but fruition, that Nancy fulfills the promise Rose made but couldn't keep. As for his tears, if they are portents of gratitude and healing, they are simply the preliminary impregnation.

Thus there are at least two interpretations possible, and we begin to suspect, in contemplating these alternative readings, that we tend to choose the one or the other according to our own lights, that in the rose glow it is ourselves that we behold.

I choose neither one nor the other, but both. It seems to me Green's triumph that he has inseparably mingled the two. Charley's past will not finally and completely die, yet it can be transcended by being joined to a viable present with a future. His tears may indicate residual instability, but they also connote release, and the sensitivity they bespeak augurs a relationship of promise. If, finally, the religious symbolism points back at betrayal and separation, it points toward resurrection.

It is Nancy as encompassing woman who, by her reaction, contains and mingles all the meanings. She can tolerate the ambiguity. Open-eyed, she accepts the responsibility of the relationship, knows what she's getting into, and finds it neither more nor less than she'd expected. She can cope, and she will help him to.

Finally, the moment to Charley cannot but be, on balance, one of great healing and union. In this instant the maimed man is made whole, his dead heart reborn. Mingling the sexual and spiritual, his final Dantesque vision of roses suggests that his love has found expression, object, and union. For him at the end, as for Eliot, the fire and the rose are one.

That sort of resolution stands in stark contrast to what we find in *Concluding* (1948), in some ways the most unresolved of the novels. There seems to be, in this story of a day in the life of old Mr. Rock, a heavy weariness that is more than his own. Perhaps it is the joyless apathy of the welfare state which is the context of the novel. It is a world of Official Reports and Official Purpose, and all the other capitalizations of a bureaucracy as dehumanized as that of Kafka's castle, in which the only thing really sacred is the status quo. The center of the story is a training institute for girls who will be government workers. The institute has taken over a large country estate, in a cottage of which lives old Mr. Rock with his granddaughter Elizabeth, now in her thirties, who is re-covering from a nervous collapse. She has rallied sufficiently to be voraciously in love with Sebastian Birt, an economics tutor, some half-dozen years and inches short of her. Rock divides his time between worrying about Elizabeth's alliance and caring for his three animals: Daisy, a sow whose lethargy informs the book and suggests the inertia of the state, Ted, his goose, and Alice, his cat. Rock, at one time a distinguished scientist, is up for an award of recognition involving a living at a sanitorium, but he and we never learn if he receives it, for he won't open his mail.

That he will receive it and leave is the fond hope of Edge. She and her sister spinster Baker are the Principals of the institution. Edge wants Rock out of there, and she is not par-ticular how. She is not above making unsavory insinuations about him and his relationship to the institute girls. Baker, less aggressive and more sympathetic than Edge, is nevertheless dominated by her.

Rock, however, lives up to his name by refusing to budge, and Edge cannot concentrate on mounting her heavy artillery against him, for she is distracted by a scandal within the institution. Two of the girls, Merode and Mary, have disappeared. Merode turns up with a flimsy story about sleepwalking, which subsequently becomes the capitalized Official Version, but Mary never reappears. Edge, the true bureaucrat, covers it up, and we never find out what happened to Mary. She may have eloped and lived happily after. On the other hand, she may have been murdered.

Edge is not the only one after Rock's cottage. Birt, if he marries Elizabeth, would like to move in. But Rock, whose morning rising opens the book, goes to bed at night at the end, still firmly ensconced in the cottage. Presumably he wins out. It hasn't been a bad day, he concludes.

If the day has been satisfactory to him, it seems less so to the other characters and to the reader, for precious little has been resolved. Green, as usual, has chosen his title with care, and his use of the present participle emphasizes the tentative quality of the book. Nothing is finally concluded; everything is left dangling. Will Rock win his award and hold his cottage, or will he lose both? Will the Institute be turned into a pig farm, as a government memo implies, or is it really already one? Will Mary reappear? Who calls her in the night? What is Rock's relationship with Moira, a student who seems inordinately fond of the old man? Will Elizabeth and Birt marry? Who wrote the anonymous obscene letter to Edge? And did she really, narcotized by cigarette smoke, propose to Rock in a moment of complete contrariness? Clearly, were this a serial, there would be much to look forward to in further installments. As it is, we are left uneasily contemplating the possibility that ambiguity itself may be Green's central theme here.

To be sure, political motifs are present, for it seems clear that the book has to do with the irreconcilable conflict between the welfare of the state and the welfare of the individual. The sterility of Edge and Baker and of the Institute itself reflect the sterility of the welfare state. Rock's sow is another surrogate for the state, devouring everything in sight. Seen in a political context, the story can be construed as that of the individual, represented by Rock, holding out against the state, represented by the Institute and Edge. Rock wins out, or is still ahead at the end, and perhaps this is a hopeful estimate of man's potential for survival in a collectivized and dehumanized society. Green's title, however, prevents excessive optimism by reminding us that this may indeed be society itself in its concluding stages.

But Green's concern is larger than politics. He seems to be dealing with the central ambiguity of human experience itself. The individual is engulfed in a morass of misunderstandings and cross-purposes, adrift in a sea of uncertainty, unable to establish much in the way of communication. *Concluding* compares in this respect with *Party Going*, another novel about one day, except that it is even less resolved than the earlier novel. At least the party goers resume their trip at the end of that book, whereas Rock, like Joyce's Bloom, simply goes to bed.

The point is, though, Rock has managed to come through the day. He has coped. Green seems here to be pointing at the essential quality for self-preservation in a shifting world— ambiguity tolerance. Like some of Faulkner's heroes and like Bloom, Rock survives, and that, in the face of the forces arrayed against him, is no mean achievement, no small victory.

With seven novels under his belt, and, as it has turned out thus far, only two more to complete, Green now emerges from behind the "gathering web of insinuations" of his prose to make a few insinuations of his own. In a series of three talks during 1950–1951 on the Third Programme of the BBC, he illuminates his past method and points toward the extremes to which he will carry it in his next two novels. The aim of the novelist, he tells his listeners in the first of these talks, is "to create a life which is not. That is to say, a life which does not eat, procreate or drink, but which can live in people who are alive." Green here seems to be talking more about analogue than imitation, for art, he points out, is not representational. And how best to create this non-representational but somehow palpable image of life in literature? "Of course, by dialogue." This is the age of the spoken word. Nobody writes letters; we use the telephone instead. Communication between individuals is now almost entirely in the form of conversation. Green's view of the communication process is not naive, however. He has already indicated his view that art is not representational; communication, it then follows, is not a direct, one-to-one affair, nor is dialogue representational either. His own dialogue does not represent exactly the way people talk; it is oblique, and for a very good reason. "For if you want to create life the one way not to set about it is explanation." Life itself does not explain itself; it is oblique in its impact on us. That is why, Green tells us, the time has come for a change from traditional narrative techniques to an increased emphasis on oblique dialogue, which must "mean different things to different readers at one and the same time."

[36]

Green's next novel, *Nothing* (1950), illustrates the extremes of his theory, or so it seems. I use the latter phrase advisedly, for its governing word is one with which Green is obsessively preoccupied during the book. The word "seems" or some form thereof appears more than fifty times, together with such variant indicators of uncertainty as "appeared," "looks," "as if," and "perhaps." These qualifiers are highly functional, for this is a phenomenological novel, in which all we are given are appearances. Relying now almost entirely on the scenic method, the novel reads like a scenario. Green is careful to keep us outside his characters and we can observe only surfaces. For all we know, what lies behind or within may be, as the title reminds us—nothing.

The surface itself is one of drawing-room comedy with viable if traditional themes, such as the gulf between generations and the struggle of two women over one elusive widower. What prevents this sort of easy classification, however, is our great uncertainty about the motives of one of the principal characters, and the presence in the novel of certain macabre undertones.

Three couples are central to the story. Initially, John Pomfret, a forty-five-year-old widower, is paired with Liz Jennings, some years younger. Their relationship seems uncomplicated: Sunday lunch at a hotel, followed by Sunday afternoon in bed. Jane Weatherby's relationship with Richard Abbot is equally uncomplicated, although sexless. He is the dutiful admirer, emotionally tongue-tied; she is the complacent widow. The third couple, Mary Pomfret and Philip Weatherby, represents the younger generation. To their elders they seem prudes; their elders to them seem unbridled, profligate.

The central action of the novel consists in muddying the waters: all the relationships change. Jane Weatherby and John

Pomfret switch partners to end up together. Rumors of their affair of years before perplex Philip and Mary into wondering whether they share a common parent. Richard Abbott continues as a dutiful admirer, but now of a frustrated Liz.

The figure which emerges in central focus in all this is that of Jane Weatherby, and the central mystery is her motivation. She presides over the novel, maneuvering to separate John from Liz and Philip from Mary. She wins John for herself again after all these years, even proposing to him, and when he accepts she claims it's his idea. She is adept at putting words in other people's mouths, and at the end, if anyone can be said to have won out, it is she. The question remains of her, however—is she a well-meaning matron or a manipulative monster?

Suggestions of monstrosity accrete around her relationship with her child, Penelope, who represents the dark side of things in her family. Apparently traumatized by a mock marriage to John Pomfret which is solemnized by a cigar band, the child is shipped off to a psychologist. Jane's attitude toward her child fluctuates between callousness and over-protectiveness. The child retaliates psychically by withdrawal and, later, by sticking pins in herself, voodoo fashion, when John's incurrence of diabetes necessitates injections. It is possible that John's guilt about all of this helps draw him back to Jane at the end.

Which brings us again to the title. We have suggested its phenomenological function; it also figures in the final ironic epiphany of the novel. John and Jane, together at the end, decide their children will have to work out their own problems. As John points out condescendingly, he and Jane "can't do everything for them." He does feel responsible for Penelope, however, whom Jane has decided to send off to school. School means hockey and thick ankles, he points out. Then she'd never allow it, she says. Always knew you couldn't send her away, he says. I mean I wouldn't let her play hockey, she says.

[38]

Penelope disposed of, the two sag against each other in somnolent comfort. Is there anything at all you want, she asks? Nothing, he replies. Which, the implication is, is pretty much what he ends up with, not only nothing but nothingness. This final reverberation of the title reveals in retrospect the existential void which may be the real context of the novel. Self-centered and spiritually impoverished, the characters play out their little scenes against a backdrop of nothingness, a world devoid of spiritual values.

This may be putting it too strongly, for certainly the action of the novel is comic, even though its implications are not. In view of this jocular dimension, the title may suggest, with Jane and John an aging Beatrice and Benedick, Green's version of much ado about.

In his last novel (to this writing), *Doting* (1952), Green continues to rely exclusively upon the almost purely scenic method employed in *Nothing*. Scenic is perhaps not the proper word, for visual detail has been drastically pared, and what is left is mostly dialogue, somewhat but not quite in the manner of Ivy Compton-Burnett, but, more importantly, exactly in what Green had announced as the only proper method of the contemporary novelist.

What the dialogue reveals is that loving has vanished, leaving only doting. A shallower form of affection, laced with an offhand but pervasive lubricity, doting is what everybody in the novel except one schoolboy does.

The principal characters are Arthur and Diana Middleton and Annabel Paynton. Annabel is regularly asked out by the Middletons as a companion for their son Peter, two years her junior, on family parties when he is home from school. One of the central developments in the story is Arthur's campaign to bed Annabel. Subsidiary roles are played by Arthur's "friend"

Charles Addinsell and Annabel's "friend" Claire Belaine. The relationships are placed in quotation marks because one of the disconcerting discoveries we make in the novel is that no one hesitates to move in on a friend's territory, particularly if that territory is a bedroom.

As in *Nothing*, a woman is the center of the book. In *Doting* it is Diana Middleton, an extension of Jane Weatherby. Again we are uncertain as to motive. Possibly Diana only wishes to regenerate their marriage by keeping Arthur off guard, anxious, guilty, and otherwise incapable of following his traditional routine of disappearing evenings with his briefcase into his study.

If this is her aim, she succeeds, for rather ironically, in the course of her bullying, threats, lies, and intrigues, their own sex life appears to increase notably in frequency if not in quality.

But Green's theme is undoubtedly more than marital regeneration. Indeed, we are not absolutely certain that that takes place, for at the end of the novel Arthur and Diana are grumbling at each other, and as Green adds, "The next day they all went on very much the same." Diana's motives seem larger if murkier. She wants her world run her way and will brook no opposition. She punishes Arthur in many subtle and unsubtle ways for his interest in young Diana. She uses Charles to make Arthur jealous. She eggs Charles on to Diana, but then blocks that relationship when it threatens to cost her Charles' loyalty. When he turns to Claire she tries to block that too. Alternatively she is procuress, philanderess, and punisher, as it suits her purpose, whatever that is. And she does all this with the constant air of the aggrieved and long-suffering wife. She may be Green's means of pushing a matriarchal theme: woman, using sex and guilt as weapons, always holds the upper hand. Certainly her favorite indoor sport seems to be pushing Arthur around. Or she may be simply Green's version of a bitch in the manger.

Some of the considerable comedy in the novel consists of poking fun at the idea of the sophisticated marriage. Arthur and Diana have agreed that each may go out if the other is not invited. In fact, this civilized arrangement does not sit very well with either of them, and is the cause of most of their problems. When Arthur, however, suggests that they quit going out with other people, Diana, with elegant if indiscernible logic, says that would indicate that their marriage had failed. Another agreement of this civilized relationship is that of mutual honesty. "Di and I don't fib to each other," says Arthur. In fact, they lie to each other almost daily, and to others about each other. Additionally ironic is Arthur's sense of marital values. He seems to be less annoyed at his wife going out with others than he is at the thought of her discussing him with others. "There must be a sort of standard of loyalty in married life, when all's said and done," he bursts out indignantly.

The final irony is that most of Arthur's lubricity toward Annabel and Diana's toward Charles is simply sex in the head. Neither Arthur or Diana is ultimately unfaithful to the other, in spite of all the jockeyings toward bedrooms. It is Charles Addinsell who finally emerges as the sly and successful fox. Charles' philosophy is simple; never love someone, she may die on you (as in fact his wife had), and then where would you be? He is, then, a confirmed doter. Unable to make the grade with Diana or Annabel, he shifts to Claire with equanimity. He and she size each other up in short order and pop off to bed together, leaving both Diana and Annabel furious at such infidelity to them.

If motive is ambiguous in this novel, so is method. On the surface, Green relies almost exclusively on the dialogue in his scenes to advance plot and convey meaning. Yet before very long one senses a curious counterpoint at work. The tenor of the narrative comment with which Green concludes his scenes is often in direct contrast to that of the dialogue itself. For example, Arthur and Diana may quarrel throughout a scene, or may be generally at odds with each other, but Green concludes by telling us that they then cheerfully discussed other topics, and so to bed smiling. Arthur and Annabel, lugubrious over their situation throughout a scene, afterward, Green tells us, suddenly become quite animated and gay, cracking jokes and so off to their respective offices smiling. This method, also employed in *Nothing*, is considerably more noticeable in *Doting*. It seems to warn us away from a purely phenomenological reading by suggesting that appearances are frequently deceiving, that things may not be at all what they seem, and that, as Green points out in his BBC talks, the same event may be interpreted quite differently by different observers, and that the way to learn about people is by watching what they do after they have spoken. In this case the gulf between what they say and what they do afterward induces an uncertainty about the whole thing, which seems to be exactly what Green has in mind in this, his last novel to date.

His silence, like his writing, is cryptic. Does he feel that the present age is too discursive for the symbolist novel? It may be that Green vanishes when Snow lies all about.

What sort of conclusions (or should they be called concludings?) does our examination of Green's work suggest? Most readily apparent is his astonishing versatility, manifesting itself in the wide range of subjects and characters in his fiction. One of Green's most remarkable achievements is the psychological verisimilitude throughout: all his characters are credible. He is particularly skilled, it seems to me, at dealing with working-class characters, and is often able to change our initial perception of them by revealing unexpected depth and dignity. As might be expected, he uses a variety of styles commensurate with this sort of diversity. At times style obtrudes and seems excessively mannered, as in *Living*. For the most part, however, style matches and serves subject.

If subjects and characters vary, basic method does not. Indeed, the perception of his consistency of method corrects the sort of misunderstanding which pictures Green sailing along successfully, relying upon his astonishingly apt instincts, until he started rationalizing them with literary theory in the BBC talks. Having articulated theory, this version continues, he was led astray by it, down the side road of *Nothing* and *Doting*, with most unfortunate results.

This interpretation does not square with what can be observed as Green's method from the beginning. It is essentially one of visual fragmentation in which he deals, for the most part, in short scenes, sometimes very short indeed, in which the essential complexes of thought and feeling seem so completely embodied that little or no expository comment is furnished or necessary.

The method varies only in degree from book to book, but is first used in his first book, in which journal entries interspersed with short scenes are the fragments. The process is violently telescoped or condensed in *Living;* the fragments are shorter and more abruptly juxtaposed, suggesting the harsh fragmentation of the lives of the workers. In *Back* there is also extreme condensation, suggesting the reductive and disintegrative aspects of war.

The technique he employs in *Nothing* and *Doting*, then, is simply another version of his method. Dialogue now replaces

[43]

image and shoulders the burden of meaning. If *Nothing* and *Doting* are inferior novels, the problem is not one of abrupt shift to less successful method. Rather, it may have been one of weakening of creative power. We must remember that Green had been carrying on two disparate careers simultaneously for more than twenty years, and diminishment of energy would seem inevitable. In addition, the subject matter of *Nothing* and *Doting* seems, by comparison, trivial, and only with difficulty do we summon that kind of involvement with character and situation which presses upon us in the best of Green's work. I think it highly significant that for the first time in these two novels, Green repeated himself, writing twice about the same sorts of characters, and in much the same fashion. He had, it would appear, worked a thin vein out.

The themes communicated through Green's novels are, as in his method, consistent, and a central one is the problem of communication itself. Misunderstandings abound in his books, as do conversations at cross-purposes and other evidences of the difficulty in striking through to establish meaningful relationships. Yet side by side with these difficulties is Green's emphasis upon the importance of communication, which should correct the interpretation of him as a wilfully or even playfully obscure writer. In his BBC talks he stresses the need for communication; in his fiction he embodies it. The communication between John Haye and Joan Entwhistle in *Blindness*, imperfect though it may be, helps John round the corner. The communication among the characters of *Party Going* is trivial but they cling to it; it represents the only organizational principle of their otherwise empty lives. It is their only defense against engulfment in the void.

Communication, in the form of loving in the novel of that name, is given its most overt endorsement as man's best chance of finding meaning in his life. The communication Charley Summers is finally able to establish in *Back* with Nancy Whittmore as herself restores him. And it is the absence of meaningful communication among the characters of Green's last two novels that sets the irony of these books, depending as they do almost entirely upon that primary agent of human communication, speech, and which gives us occasional disheartening glimpses of the empty skull beneath the skin of comedy.

We have already noted individual examples and here need only remind ourselves of another important aspect of his work, the achievement of what might be called connectedness of structure, or pervasiveness of central idea. Green achieves this elusive quality by his choice of titles, which seem, to an unusual degree, to sum up his novels. In almost every instance, and this is particularly true with the participial titles, all of the characters are in various ways participating in the kind of action the title describes. But he also uses the kind of structural device we have identified in several of his novels. The water in *Blindness*, various kinds of birds in *Living*, *Party Going*, and *Loving*, roses in *Back*—all of these symbolic agents perform the same general function as his titles: to order, to connect, to bind together.

Ironically, what is bound together is frequently the void. There is a curious emptiness in Green's fictional world, a prevalent sense of nothingness, to be bridged if possible, but always there. Clearly, the spiritual dimension is missing in the world he describes; God is, if not dead, absent. And yet, there is always the hint or at least the possibility of renewal, which is the closest Green comes to any sort of recognizable affirmation. Haye in *Blindness*, Lily in *Living*, Roe in *Caught*, Raunce in *Loving*, and Summers in *Back* are all characters who seem to be, at the end of their respective novels, on the verge of rebirth of a sort, on the threshold of reintegration and consequent regeneration. In each case, this renewal depends on the ability of the individual to come to terms with himself and his situation, to confront and accept at a stroke past, present, and future, and to accept and tolerate the ambiguities inherent in all three.

Ambiguity is where we started with Green, and where we end. Above all, what he shows us in his fiction is the imponderable variegation of human experience in an ultimately cryptic cosmos. Like Conrad, Green sees an undecipherable world; like Joyce, who coined the word, he sees a jocoserious world. Joy and sorrow intermingle, as do the lovely and the grotesque, sanity and dementia, love and lovelessness.

Ambiguity is not there simply for its own sake, but because, as Green has pointed out, life itself does not explain, and the writer trying to create life must not either. Human experience, after all, is one discrepancy after the other; its central aspects are complex and undecipherable. All writers know that, of course. The difference between Green and many of them is that they, having assumed this, write their novels as if it were not so. Green, on the other hand, writes as if it were exactly so, and the whole point.

"We shall never know the truth," says old Rock in *Concluding*. Yeats, who said man can embody truth but cannot know it, would certainly concur with Rock. But Rock and we have to go on living, and to Green, one's main source of viability is ambiguity tolerance, or as Keats put it better, the negative capability. It is this ability to exist in doubt and certainty that, in Green's view, carries us on, and is the only thing that will. For in Green's world as in ours, all in the end is uncertain. He makes us certain of that.

[46]

SELECTED BIBLIOGRAPHY

PRINCIPAL WORKS BY HENRY GREEN

Blindness. London, J. M. Dent, 1926; New York, E. P. Dutton, 1926.

Living. London, Hogarth Press, 1929; New York, Macmillan, 1929.

Party Going. London, Hogarth Press, 1939; New York, Viking Press, 1951.

Pack My Bag. London, Hogarth Press, 1940.

Caught. London, Hogarth Press, 1943; New York, Viking Press, 1950.

Loving. London, Hogarth Press, 1945; New York, Viking Press, 1949.

Back. London, Hogarth Press, 1946; New York, Viking Press, 1950.

Concluding. London, Hogarth Press, 1948; New York, Viking Press, 1950.

Nothing. London, Hogarth Press, 1950; New York, Viking Press, 1950.

Doting. London, Hogarth Press, 1952; New York, Viking Press, 1952.

"A Novelist to his Readers: Communication without Speech," *The Listener*, November 9, 1950.

"A Novelist to his Readers—II," *The Listener*, March 15, 1951.

"A Fire, a Flood, and the Price of Meat," *The Listener*, August 23, 1951.

"For Jenny with Affection from Henry Green," *Spectator*, October 4, 1963.

CRITICAL WORKS AND COMMENTARY

Dennis, Nigel. "The Double Life of Henry Green," *Life*, August 4, 1952.

Hall, James, "The Fiction of Henry Green: Paradoxes of Pleasure-and-Pain," *Kenyon Review*, Winter, 1957.

Melchiori, Giorgio. The Tightrope Walkers. London, Routledge and Kegan Paul, 1956.

Phelps, Robert. "The Vision of Henry Green," *The Hudson Review*, Winter, 1953.

Russell, John. Henry Green: Nine Novels and an Unpacked Bag. New Brunswick, Rutgers University Press, 1960.

———. "There It Is," *Kenyon Review*, Summer, 1964.

Southern, Terry. "Henry Green" (interview), *Paris Review,* Summer, 1958.

Stokes, Edward. The Novels of Henry Green. London, The Hogarth Press, 1959.

Tindall, William Y. Forces in Modern British Literature, 1885–1956. New York, Vintage Books, 1956.

———. The Literary Symbol. New York, Columbia University Press, 1955.

Toynbee, Philip. "The Novels of Henry Green," *Partisan Review,* May, 1949.

Weatherhead, A. Kingsley. A Reading of Henry Green. Seattle, University of Washington Press, 1961.

Welty, Eudora. "Henry Green: A Novelist of the Imagination," *Texas Quarterly,* Autumn, 1961.

COLUMBIA ESSAYS ON MODERN WRITERS

EDITOR: William York Tindall

ADVISORY EDITORS:
Jacques Barzun, W.T.H. Jackson, Joseph A. Mazzeo, Justin O'Brien

Each pamphlet, 65 cents. Orders accepted only for 6 or m pamphlets, same or assorted titles.

Distributed in the United Kingdom and in Europe by Columbia University Press, Ltd., 70 Great Russell Street, London W.(U.K. price: 5s net

Order from your bookseller or from

COLUMBIA UNIVERSITY PRESS
Irvington, New York 10533